Little notes to myself:

Copyright © 2022 by Santiego Rivers

ssrivers.com / Amazon

One of the most valuable lessons life has taught me was that my dreams are my responsibility.

Before making myself accountable for the good and not-so-good moments in my life, I blamed everyone for me not having or being where I wanted to be in my life.

In the midst of my storms, I forgot who I was, but more importantly, I forgot to whom I belonged.

Once my mind came to grips with what my soul knew, I was determined to use everything others meant to break me to make me stronger.

With pen in hand, I began to write. I wrote about the good, the bad, and even those indifferences that made me pause and think.

I used everything I wondered about to help bring clarity into my life. A writer knows that your visions will never manifest in your life until you write them down.

Each affirmation I wrote and learned from became another tool I put into my toolbox to help me become the person God intended me to be.

From this book, take what you need and leave what you don't. I hope you take the following and apply it to your life.

You cannot heal in the same environment that hurt you.

If you let it, your pain can teach you lessons you are not prepared to learn.

A person will change if properly motivated

I needed peace in my life!

I was tired of always being angry, upset, mad, and frustrated because of how I felt inside.

I felt that my life was spinning out of control.

It took me a long time to learn that I was in complete control of the outcome regarding the good and the bad things that happened in my life.

Even a fool will eventually learn if they live long enough that it is never about the situations in your life; instead, how you respond to your life's problems matters the most.

Learning to accept that affirmation made me ready to be the change that my life needed.

While learning to accept that everything I faced was for my betterment brought me closer to God and is helping me to find peace in my life.

During my time of growth, I grew to understand that God is not committed to fulfilling our dreams. Instead, he is committed to us fulfilling his purpose for our life.

Finding clarity came when I learned to replace my anger with patience and acceptance, which allowed me to focus on the things that would help bring peace to my life.

After years of denial, I have come to accept that God will use people and situations to help teach you lessons that will eventually develop you for the best.

I became inspired to develop a peaceful mindset instead of continuing to war with myself.

What I decided to do every day I woke up was write a note to myself to help encourage me and keep me motivated throughout my day.

These short notes gave me something to think about and reminded me that God is always in control, even when it feels like my life is out of control.

I had to learn and accept that if it's big enough to worry about, it's big enough to pray about.

Doing this daily task helped me start my day with an attitude of gratitude. I now had a reason to smile.

Please write it down!

Writing it down helped remove a lot of things in my mind

The best way to manifest the thoughts in your head is to write them down. It is easier to forget the ideas in your head compared to the things you have to look at throughout the day.

Writing things down made me accountable for ensuring I completed the task or stayed mindful that I was working on something significant.

I feel that when you learn to hold yourself accountable for your actions or lack thereof, it helps you keep the power you give to others by shying away from your responsibility.

Changing your life for the better is your responsibility. Your parents gave you life. It is your job to determine what you decide to do with the life God blessed you to have.

Even when you may feel it is not, life is a blessing!

If you learn to utilize your vision, you can achieve anything your mind can imagine. Images and words give your imagination permission to flourish. Put them on paper!

It doesn't become real until you write it down.

For years, I carried dreams in my mind, which over time became nightmares because I was not doing all I could to help manifest them in my life.

What if I failed? What if I was not good enough to accomplish it? Self-doubt destroys more chances of success than trying and not succeeding.

It took me some time to learn, but eventually, I realized the following:

Just because it's tough, it doesn't mean it is impossible.

At an early age, I fell in love with writing. Writing allowed me to express myself in ways my spoken words could not at that time of my life.

Through my writing, I found the voice of my soul that gave me the courage to stop using the pain of my heart to express myself.

Who knew the skills I developed as a child would later save the adult version of me who was still carrying the baggage the child should have put down long ago?

Everything we need to change our life for the better is already within our reach. We need to learn to stop looking outwards for the things God put within us to become the best version of ourselves.

The first thing I wrote down on paper at the lowest point of my life is **why**.

Why?

The answer to this straightforward question

would help me change my life for the better.

Unfortunately, I would not come to understand the answer to that question for a very long time in my life, but I eventually did.

Each person must discover the answer to that question on their own for them to accept the answer.

You can reject them if someone else is providing you with answers. However, it is not until you discover it for yourself that you will be ready to process and accept the results you have found.

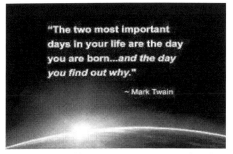

I have discovered and accepted both!

After being able to answer my **"Why"** question, it led me to tackle the next thing on my agenda.

Stop looking for the version of yourself that makes sense to the world. Instead, discover the version of you that makes you happy.

I spent most of my life trying to become the version of myself that would make me loveable to others simply because I lacked self-love.

I spent so much time trying to fit in with people, not realizing and accepting God created me to stand out.

I spent so much time being a chameleon that it made it hard to recognize my reflection when I looked in the mirror.

So much time… So much time… Time is the only thing we can lose that we can never get back, but we still waste so much time.

Each version of myself I created to fit in with others gave me what I wanted at the moment, but it never gave me the one thing I needed to sustain myself.

When I wrote the note to myself to stop looking for the version of myself that makes sense to the world but instead discover the version of me that made me happy, a smile came over my face.

Putting those words on paper gave me what I needed to put those words into action in my life.

I realized that if I was unhappy with myself, how could anyone else give me what I was unwilling to show myself?

No one can do for you what you're unwilling to do for yourself. So I have realized that the people we try to impress or make happy are miserable.

Your happiness with yourself will change your life in ways you'll never imagine.

Fight all your battles with prayer.

I wrote myself this note to remind me that God never intended for me to face any adversity alone.

I held everything inside for a long time because I did not know who I could trust or who cared enough to listen to me.

When facing adversity, it becomes easy to feel like we are alone even when we are surrounded by people who would gladly help us, with no strings attached.

It's not easy to trust others when we have been hurt by those close to us. But, we will never heal from the things we are unwilling to face.

Everything we go through is necessary. Every testimony requires a test. You can't ask for strength but are unwilling to face situations that will make you stronger.

The most challenging thing I had to do was learn to take all my trouble and worries to God.

I have found that dropping to my knees in prayer has helped me stay out of jail, prison, and even the cemetery.

For me, prayer changes things, but you must be willing to do it for it to work. What prayer has done for me is more than my pride, anger, and stubbornness have ever done.

I often look back on this note to remind me what to do when my problems are more than I can handle alone.

Stop complaining about the situation you're currently in and start asking yourself what you can learn from it.

Nightmares don't make pretty dreams, but that does not mean you cannot learn from them if you're willing to learn.

Every time I faced adversity in my life, I always wondered why me, lord. Why was I facing so much hardship in my life? Instead of realizing I was blessed to be in a situation to learn important lessons for my life.

God never promised us the lack of adversity in our life. But, he always guaranteed us that we would not face them alone.

When you fight all your battles with prayer, it gives you a different perspective on the problems that occur in life.

On my journey to self-discovery, I realized that the blessing is always inside the lesson.

Once I stopped complaining about everything I was going through, it allowed me to learn from the situations I was facing.

I learned that you could never appreciate the value of peace without knowing the hardship of war.

Nor could you respect the gift of love without knowing the struggles of pain. I don't claim to be some great philosopher. I know that I got to a point where my way of doing things was not working in my best interest.

For a man to change, it often takes shaking the foundation on which he stands. We often find it easier to go to war with others than to have a duel with ourselves.

I am not telling you what I think. I am merely telling you what I know because I have lived every word.

The reason I can talk about it is that I have lived it.

Experience is the best teacher, especially for those who love learning but do not always like being taught.

I cannot tell you what it's like to play professional sports or go to the moon because I am not a professional athlete or an astronaut.

I can tell you all about what it's like to cry yourself to sleep at night, and when the morning comes, you stop mourning and start surviving.

Becoming a survivor will not occur overnight. It is a process that will be very grueling and demanding, but it will be worth it in the end.

A survivor learns to use the things meant to break them to make them stronger mentally.

For me, it started with a mirror and a heart-to-soul conversation that went the following way:

"I have been called everything under the sun but a child of God. I have  been lied to, betrayed, and used. I have been made to feel I was powerless to change the things that were happening to me. I can't count the times I cried to sleep or prayed that God had mercy on me and called me home. I have been knocked to my knees so many times I wondered why I don't just remain there. Once I could finally stop crying and remain silent, a voice from within asked me one simple question. *(Why?)* **Everything you need is already within you, so why not use what you have to get what you want and need?**"

Sometimes *"reality checks"* will hit you harder than any punch or kick could. Therefore, I used the ammunition other people used against me to help build me back up.

I was determined to be everything they said I wasn't or couldn't be.

Little notes to myself became very significant blocks for building my foundation.

Each note was a missing piece of the puzzle I needed to help make me hold. Only when you combine **faith** with your **hard work** will you be able to see the results that will help change your life for the better.

It wasn't easy to get on my current path. There were many setbacks, but I made sure that my attempts to succeed were more than my setbacks.

Please re-read that section as often as needed for it to register in your heart and soul.

I learned long ago that it is okay for people to see you mess up; just don't let them see you quit.

Your attempts at success should not be for anyone but yourself. But unfortunately, I do admit letting "**Haters**" see what their "**hating**" has produced is **AMAZING**!

I want to live in peace, not pieces

For years, I had felt like an incomplete puzzle because I allowed people to come into my life and take pieces of me when they left.

When a giver does not have a limit to what they're willing to give, it allows takers to keep taking until there's nothing left.

Good intentions turn sour when that one special part of you, blessed by God, is used against you; your caring heart.

We let people inside our sacred place whose only intention is to use, hurt, and destroy because it makes them feel better about themselves.

Some people would insist on taking things from you that you would gladly give

because it is your nature to give.

Others will use your giving heart to leave it broken into pieces.

Heartache and pain will force you to pause and think about the situations in your life that have dropped you to your knees.

It was one thing my mother taught me long ago, which took a while to understand and use in my life, but when I finally did it, I could start putting myself back together again.

"The letter (I) comes before the letter (U) in the dictionary."

I had to learn to be about making myself whole and feeling complete before I could help anyone else.

Who will take care of me but myself when I need assistance?

My mindset had to become the following if I planned to rescue myself from myself because we are the only problem and solution in our lives.

"I'm all about (I), so you can keep them other vowels."

That concept is challenging for a caring and giving person to accept and apply to their life, but pain and heartache will make you do whatever it takes to have peace in your life.

Learn to put yourself first!

Don't expect other people to do for you what you're unwilling to do for yourself.

Putting yourself first may sound selfish to some people, but it is the remedy for those trying to heal and protect their peace of mind.

You will never heal from the things you're unwilling to face.

You will forever be missing valuable pieces of yourself until you learn to make some tough decisions about saving your life. Your job is not to get other people to understand and accept why you're doing what's best for you. Your primary job is to make sure you know your reasons.

You won't know how good it is to feel whole until you have been broken.

What will it take to survive both mentally and physically?

Surviving life's obstacles will cost whatever it costs; you must be willing to pay it regardless.

Your new life will cost you your old life, but it's worth it. If your old life could get you to your desired destination, it would have gotten you there.

Paying the price for becoming the best version of myself is the testimony my tests in life have allowed me to share with those looking to be inspired.

My journey to the here and now was not easy, but I made sure that my rough roads led to a beautiful destination. Every step I took, I reminded myself of one simple thing.

On the back end of quitting is a lifetime of regrets.

Stop allowing your past to defeat you

Your past should only be a teaching tool to help guide your future. It would be best if you never allowed it to get you stuck in a place you've outgrown.

A valuable lesson I learned that helped me improve my ability to focus was the following.

We will move in the direction we focus on.

Where is your focus taking you in your life? I hope it's not in your past. God would allow anything in your past to be in your life if it was needed for your future.

Stop holding onto memories that do not inspire you to keep moving forward with your life. Time is the one thing we waste too much of that we can never get back.

Stop trying to play God and then wondering why things are not working in your favor.

Wanting stuff from our past or remembering bad memories from it will take away from us realizing the gift we have today. What gift, you may wonder.

Today is the gift, which is why it's called the **PRESENT**. God never promised us tomorrow. So all we have is *today*.

Today gives us the opportunity to right any wrong from our past by not allowing it to steal or sabotage our future.

What is meant to be will be, so let it be.

Your desires will work against you if you try to force them to manifest in your life. Your fears will also work against you, making you afraid to keep moving forward.

When it comes to people:

There is one thing for certain and two things for sure.

There will be people who only see your flaws and not the greatness within you. Be sure not to be one of those people.

There are those who've helped you, left you, and put you through difficult times. You must be willing to let go of anyone who is not working with you, only against you.

Most people in our lives take away from us more than they can provide.

Let them Go! Hold on to something worth holding onto, like your *Self-Respect, dignity*, and *self-love*.

Will those people you leave in your past be mad at you? How someone else feels about you is none of your concern. Their actions made them expendable.

Care more about protecting your peace than your name to those who will only use it in vain.

Keep moving in the direction you desire to go.

They cannot curse what God has blessed.

If the people around you are not building you up, they are part of the reason you are breaking down.

Only you can give them the power to affect what you decide to do with your life.

I learned the hard way, but I eventually learned no one would respect you if you kept giving them the opportunity to disrespect you.

You can't build with someone unwilling to help you carry the bricks.

Stop running back to the same people who tried to break you. If they turned their back on you, ensure they keep it turned away from you.

Stop trying to move mountains for those who won't appreciate your effort. Most people will never respect you when you're giving them your all, but they will notice and be upset when you stop trying to please them and focus on making yourself happy.

Stop destroying yourself by trying to hurt the people who hurt you. The energy and time you spend on getting even with the people who've wronged you take away the energy and time you could have spent on getting peace in your life.

Stop letting people change you for the worse. The walls you build to protect your heart from hurt and pain will also prevent you from truly being loved.

Don't allow anyone to make you jeopardize the **blessing** and **favor** God has for your life. Instead, let God fight the battle, and you focus on maintaining your peace.

No one can stop you but you!

If there's no enemy within, the enemy outside can do you no harm.

I repeat that mantra whenever worry and fear attempt to invade one of my most valuable assets. **(My mind)**

I have realized that worry and fear only come knocking when we forget God is in complete control.

I did not always have the ability to pause and think, which affected my ability to see past my worries.

Our mind becomes quicksand when we allow negative thoughts to become the  things that fill our heads.

Our unwanted feelings make us act in ways that lead us to a downward spiral we cannot control.

How do we begin to trust our actions when we cannot even depend on our state of mind because fear and doubt have replaced our confidence and ability to stay positive?

What we feel becomes how we react when our actions are based on negativity. When we think that all hope is gone, it makes it easy for us to stop trying.

 Victory seems impossible, so we give up trying because our efforts seem useless.

Facing my fears and doubts gave me the following understanding that inspired me to do the one thing I thought was impossible: **Keep Fighting**!

Without effort, things will die that God wanted to live.

Never quit fighting for the things you **want** because the things you **need** to improve your life will take all your effort.

Before you created plans for yourself, God had a purpose for your life. Therefore, Throw away any list you made that God was not a part of creating.

The hardest part of accomplishing your goals will be sacrificing your pride, but be sure of one important thing.

It won't change you for the better if it doesn't challenge you.

Each little note I wrote and posted, any and everywhere I could, reminded me of the thing my troubles and fears almost made me forget. **I am enough!**

It's never about how things start or currently going. It's about how you finish that matters.

I am nowhere close to my final destination, but I appreciate everything the journey teaches me along the way.

I hope this book will remind you that you are enough and allow you to keep moving forward.

Made in the USA
Columbia, SC
26 October 2022

70052421R00022